EVERYDAY GUIDES

MADE EASY

MIXING FOR COMPUTER MUSICIANS

Publisher's note: The conversion rate from US dollars (USD) to British pound sterling (GBP) at the time of publishing was 1 USD = 1.6 GBP. The conversion rate for Euro to GBP was 1 Euro = 0.73 GBP.

This is a **FLAME TREE** book
First published 2015

Publisher and Creative Director: Nick Wells
Project Editor: Polly Prior
Art Director and Layout Design: Mike Spender
Digital Design and Production: Chris Herbert
Copy Editor: Karen Fitzpatrick
Technical Editor: Stephen Evans
Proofreader: Dawn Laker
Indexer: Helen Snaith
Screenshots: Ronan Macdonald

Special thanks to: Gillian Whitaker, Josie Mitchell and Laura Bulbeck

This edition first published 2015 by
FLAME TREE PUBLISHING
Crabtree Hall, Crabtree Lane
Fulham, London SW6 6TY
United Kingdom

www.flametreepublishing.com

15 17 19 18 16
1 3 5 7 9 10 8 6 4 2

© 2015 Flame Tree Publishing

ISBN 978-1-78361-412-7

All non-screenshot pictures are: courtesy of Alesis and © 2015 inMusic Brands, Inc: 11t.; Copyright © 2015 LOUD Technologies Inc.: 25; © 2015 Livid Shop: 27; courtesy of Shutterstock.com and © the following contributors: Dmitry Nikolaev 1 ; Onigiri studio 3 ; Mihai Simonia 5 ; bikeriderlondon 6 ; Vladimir Gramagin 7 ; Maciej Czekajewski 8 ; nikkytok 10 ; nikkytok 11b; Michael Photo 12 ; Agorohov 13 ; Dmitry Elagin 14 ; klyuchnikovart 15 ; wavebreakmedia 23 ; Goodluz 26 ; vyskoczilova 28 ; Kerdkanno 32 ; Aschindl 34; Be Good 35; Darrin Henry 36; Devin_Pavel 42; Asier Romero 44; exopixel 46; sfam_photo 48; I love photo 50; Zarya Maxim Alexandrovich 54; StockLite 56; optimarc 60; Phoric 62; BlueSkyImage 66; Aaron Amat 68; Glovatskiy 69; Cameron Whitman 74; 4736202690 76; Kzenon 79; Blend Images 81; Janaka Dharmasena 86; ArtvarkFilm 102; Eillen 104; Hteam 105; Pimnana_01 106; Svetlana Larina 107; Di Studio 108; portumen 110; NEGOVURA 115; wavebreakmedia 115; Deni_M 122; nmedia 126; courtesy of Wikimedia Commons and the following: JacoTen 112; Masterplus 125.

EVERYDAY GUIDES
MADE EASY

MIXING FOR COMPUTER MUSICIANS

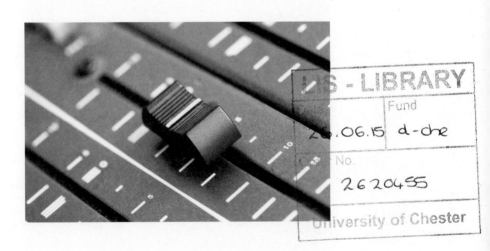

RONAN MACDONALD

FLAME TREE
PUBLISHING

CONTENTS

Discover the hardware and software you need to get up and running
with computer-based mixing.

Take a tour of the mixer and establish your basic sound field by setting
levels and pan positions.

Control the volume and frequency shaping of your mix using compression,
limiting, gating and EQ plug-ins.

Reverb, delay, distortion and more are covered, as we show you how
to take your mix to the next sonic level.

A grab bag of things to consider and try as you approach and execute your mixes.

When the mixing's done, the mastering engineer takes over.
Whether that's you or someone else, here's what you need to know.

SERIES FOREWORD

While the unstoppable rise of computer technology has left no area of the creative arts untouched, perhaps the most profoundly transformed of them all is music. From performance, composition and production to marketing, distribution and playback, the Apple Mac and Windows PC – and, more recently, their increasingly capable smartphone and tablet cousins – have given anyone, no matter what their budget, the ability to produce professional-quality tracks in the comfort of their own home and put them online for the whole world to hear.

Virtual studios like Logic Pro and Pro Tools (and the software instruments and effects that plug into them) put more audio and MIDI recording, editing, processing and mixing power at your fingertips than even their most well-equipped real-world counterparts could have hoped to match only 20 years ago. What's rather more difficult to come by though is the knowledge required to put all that good stuff to use – which is where this book comes in.

A comprehensive guide to mixing, taking you through all the key concepts in a succinct, easy-to-understand way, *Mixing For Computer Musicians* is sure to serve as a trusty companion on your music-making journey, whether you're a total beginner or a more advanced producer looking to brush up on the basics. Work through it methodically from start to finish, or keep it by your side for reference – just don't forget to give us a credit on your debut album.

Ronan Macdonald
Music technology writer and editor

INTRODUCTION

Mixing is the most esoteric, technical and creatively rewarding stage of the music production process. This book gives the computer musician all the knowledge they need to get started.

NEED TO KNOW

Filled with practical advice, this book will guide you through the basics of mixing, explaining every stage of the process in plain English, and giving specific advice to help you become a better mix engineer.

SMALL CHUNKS

There's a lot to cover, so we've boiled the info in this book down to the essentials. Each chapter is broken down into short sections, keeping everything clear and succinct, and enabling you to dip in and out as you need to.

STEP-BY-STEP GUIDES

These walk you through a range of mixing techniques, from bussing and mid/side processing to compression and EQ.

Hot Tips

Look out for Hot Tips throughout the book – bite-size techniques and ideas to try and consider.

SIX CHAPTERS

This book is divided up into six chapters. The first is something of a buyer's guide, guiding you through the equipment and software you need to set up your mixing environment. The second chapter addresses the very basics of mixing – volume and panning – as well as mid/side processing. Chapter three steps things up a technical notch as we get into dynamics and EQ, while chapter four looks at employing mixing effects of various kinds. Chapter five presents a collection of food-for-thought mixing tips, before chapter six wraps up with an overview of the processes involved in producing the final master.

GEARING UP

MONITORING

The quality of your monitoring set-up is of crucial importance at the mixdown stage. A decent pair of speakers is a must, as is an acoustically reliable mixing environment.

ACTIVE OR PASSIVE?

There are two options when it comes to buying studio monitor speakers: active and passive.

Above: Be sure to buy the best monitors you can afford.

Passive Resistance

Passive monitors require an externally amplified input signal to get their drivers (woofer, tweeter, etc.) moving.

Above: Passive monitors only work in tandem with an amp.

With no built-in amplifiers adding to the component and manufacturing costs, passive monitors are a lot cheaper than their active counterparts, even when you factor in the cost of the accompanying amplifier. However, since the speaker and amp aren't designed specifically to match each other, they don't sound as good.

The Active Advantage

Active monitors have amplifiers built in (either one per driver, or a single amp powering all of the drivers), receiving input directly from the audio interface connected to your computer.

Right: Active monitors have amplifiers built in.

With the amplifier and speakers being matched by the manufacturer – i.e., designed and built to work together as a unit – you can expect an active monitor to reproduce the sound being played through it more accurately than a passive monitor at the same price point.

Active monitors range in size and price from small ones costing a few hundred pounds/dollars, to enormous ones priced at many thousands. It's well worth investing as much as you can afford to in them.

SUBWOOFER

If you want to hear the very lowest frequencies but don't have the space or budget for a pair of larger monitors, you're going to need a subwoofer.

The Sub Way

A subwoofer is a floor-standing speaker designed for the reproduction of frequencies from around 20–100 Hz. For mixes comprising real instruments (drum kit, guitar, vocals, etc.), you can probably get away without a sub, but if you're producing bass-heavy electronic music, you should strongly consider splashing out on one – preferably from the same manufacturer and series as your main monitors.

Below: If you're serious about bass, you need a sub.

HEADPHONES

As well as your monitors, a good pair of studio headphones should be on any mix engineer's shopping list.

Not a Speaker Substitute

Unless you're mixing late into the night and don't want to annoy the neighbours, headphones should never be your first choice for monitoring. Since headphones only let you hear each side of the stereo image in one ear, they can't give a realistic impression of the left/right soundstage – unlike your speakers, each of which serves its output to both ears.

Headphones come into their own, however, when you need to zoom in on the mix, appraising low-level details like reverb tails, sub-bass and background noise.

Right: A pair of headphones is an important monitoring accessory.

ACOUSTIC TREATMENT

To get your mixes sounding great, your control room needs to be up to scratch.

Changing Rooms

While the nitty-gritty of control room acoustics is beyond the scope of this book, the importance of treating your studio to get it sounding right can't be overstated. From the placement of your speakers and listening position to minimize the effect of standing waves, to the construction of bass traps and reflection absorbers on the floor, walls and ceiling to rein in overblown low frequencies and bouncing sound waves, there's quite a lot that you'll need to do before you can consider your room truly mix-worthy. It's not difficult though, and it needn't cost the earth, as an internet search for 'home studio acoustics' will reveal.

Below: Make every effort to get your room sounding good – your mixes will thank you for it.

MIXING PLUG-INS

In the last 15 years or so, software plug-ins have revolutionized the home studio, bringing powerful virtual effects to the Mac/PC digital audio workstation (DAW) at a fraction of the price of their hardware ancestors.

YOUR VIRTUAL STUDIO

Whichever software DAW you use – be it Cubase, Live, Reason, Pro Tools or one of the many others on the market – you already have everything you need to make great mixes, including a virtual mixer replicating everything you'd find on the physical equivalent, and a collection of bundled effects.

Above: Your DAW comes with its own effects, but you'll want to look further afield too.

RECOMMENDED PLUG-INS

However, when you're ready to expand on those basic devices, there's an almost overwhelming array of amazing third-party plug-ins out there to discover. Here are some notables.

Compressors

○ **DMG Audio Compassion:** Absurdly flexible dynamics plug-in that not only delivers superb compression but also gating, expansion, transient shaping and more, via a configurable topology. £149.99/$230.54, **www.dmgaudio.com**

Above: Get lost in a world of compression with DMG Audio's dynamics construction kit.

○ **FabFilter Pro-C:** Powerful program-dependent compression with sidechaining, mid/side processing, customizable routing and a good-looking display that gives excellent visual feedback on what's happening to the source signal. £124/$190.59, **www.fabfilter.com**

○ **Klanghelm DC8C:** This affordable plug-in's Easy and Expert modes offer two levels of involvement, while two saturation modes give a choice of sonic flavours. DC8C would still be a must-have at five times the price! £15.12/$21, **www.klanghelm.com**

- **Waves CLA-76**: An emulation of the classic Urei 1176 compressor/limiter – a legendary processor from the 1960s that has been used on countless records through the last five decades and proves particularly effective on drums. £260/$400, **www.waves.com**

- **Native Instruments Supercharger GT**: Designed by Softube, NI's tube-emulating plug-in sounds nothing short of incredible, with three increasingly hard-hitting modes – Mild, Crisp and Slam – making it a viable tool for any dynamics-shaping task. £89/$136, **www.native-instruments.com**

- **FXpansion DCAM FreeComp**: This circuit-modelled virtual compressor comes in at a price that can't be argued with, and really does the business on group busses and the master channel. Free, **www.fxpansion.com**

> ## Hot Tip
>
> **As well as applying compression, many compressors bring their own desirable character and identity to the sound.**

Above: Supercharger GT will send your mixes into overdrive.

Equalizers

○ **DMG Audio Equilibrium:** The EQ equivalent of their Compassion compressor, DMG's stellar plug-in is freely configurable and can operate up to 32 bands at once, drawing on a wide range of filter types. £174.99/$268.99, **www.dmgaudio.com**

○ **FabFilter Pro-Q 2:** Pro-Q 2 really pushes the envelope with its innovative Spectrum Grab feature, which lets you sculpt the sound to create an EQ curve, rather than vice versa. Amazing stuff. £124/$190.59, **www.fabfilter.com**

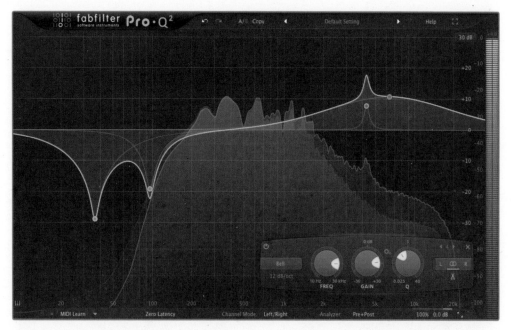

Above: Pro-Q 2 is arguably the greatest EQ plug-in ever made.

○ **PSP Audioware NobleQ:** Pultec's EQP-1A is a classic vintage hardware EQ held in high regard by engineers the world over, and PSP's emulation of it not only sounds a lot like the real thing but also extends the feature set to make it far more versatile. £44.89/$69, **www.pspaudioware.com**

- **IK Multimedia EQ 73**: Emulating the legendary Neve 1073 hardware unit, EQ 73 does a sterling job of capturing the sound and spirit of the original, right down to the virtual preamp. £72.64/$111.65, **www.ikmultimedia.com**

- **Photosounder SplineEQ**: This easy-to-use linear phase EQ plug-in uses Bézier splines to create its curves, resulting in complex, precise filter shapes that simply couldn't be realized any other way. £18.99/$29, **www.photosounder.com**

Below: Equalization doesn't get much more surgical that SplineEQ.

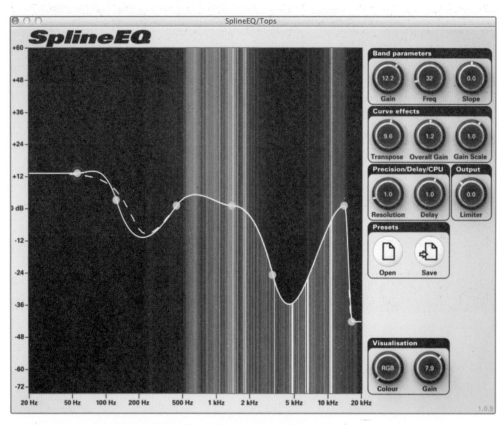

- **Blue Cat Audio Triple EQ**: A three-band semi-parametric EQ in which all three bands can be controlled together, as if they were a single filter. It's free, so you'd be mad not to. Free, **www.bluecataudio.com**

Reverb

- **2CAudio Aether**: With its dual-engine architecture (enabling discrete control of early and late reflections), plethora of ambience-shaping controls and beautiful sound, Aether can work spatial miracles in any mix. £162.62/$249.95, **www.2caudio.com**

- **Audio Ease Altiverb 7**: Based on a huge library of sampled real-world spaces and classic studio equipment, this revered convolution reverb is the one to beat when it comes to realism and sheer quality. £362/$556.30, **www.audioease.com**

Above: Want to put your singer in Notre Dame? With Altiverb, you really can!

- **ValhallaDSP VintageVerb**: Cheap and very cheerful indeed, Valhalla's Lexicon-inspired plug-in presents nine plate, room and hall algorithms – and sounds awesome. £32.53/$50, **www.valhalladsp.com**

- **UVI SparkVerb**: Boasting an ingenious preset handling system in its Voyager screen, this intuitive algorithmic reverb is an outstanding studio workhorse. £129.47/$199, **www.uvi.net**

Delay

- **D16 Sigmund**: Comprising four independent delay lines, each with its own filter, overdrive module, modulation setup and more, Sigmund is geared up for far more than just conventional echoes. £59/$90.68, **www.d16.pl**

Above: Create intricate echoes with Sigmund.

- **Soundtoys EchoBoy**: Choose from a rich variety of 30 vintage emulation delay models and design your own echo patterns with this extraordinary plug-in. £116.46/$179, **www.soundtoys.com**

- **Rob Papen RP-Delay**: RP-Delay's six delay lines and extensive feature set make it a formidable weapon in the mix engineer's arsenal. £35.60/$54.72, **www.robpapen.com**

○ **FabFilter Timeless 2:**
A stunning time-stretching
tape delay emulation with dual
filters and FabFilter's flexible
drag-and-drop modulation
system. £89/$136.76,
www.fabfilter.com

> ## Hot Tip
>
> **Many delay plug-ins can be pressed into service for chorusing, phasing and flanging, as well as echo effects.**

Channel Strips

- **iZotope Alloy 2**: Rolling EQ, transient shaping, de-essing, limiting and two powerful Dynamics modules into one plug-in, Alloy 2 is a mixing Swiss army knife with excellent metering and a dazzling sound. £129.47/$199, **www.izotope.com**

Above: iZotope Alloy: all the mixing essentials in one plug-in.

- **Wave Arts TrackPlug**: Packing everything you could want in a traditional-style channel strip into a single screen – 10-band EQ, filters, two compressors, gate/expander and limiter – TrackPlug is agile, user-friendly and sonically on point. £96.94/$149, **www.wavearts.com**

- **Solid State Logic Duende Native Channel:** It might not have the visual bells and whistles of more modernist channel strip plug-ins, but this one brings the jaw-dropping sound of the legendary SSL C200 console to your DAW. £199/$305, **www.solid-state-logic.com**

MIDI MIX CONTROLLERS

For when you want to truly connect with your mixes, the physical faders, knobs and buttons of a MIDI control surface replicate the hands-on feel of a hardware mixer.

TOTAL CONTROL

A MIDI mix controller isn't for everyone, but it's certainly something you should try.

What Are They and What's the Point?

A MIDI mix controller is a faux mixer that connects to your DAW via MIDI and lets you adjust your virtual mixer's faders, pan pots, effects, send levels etc., with its physical controls. The idea is simply to make your DAW feel more like a real studio.

But Do You Need One?

If you mix as you go, rather than approaching mixdown as a production stage in its own right (see page 32), you may not find a great deal of use for a MIDI controller, since you'll

Above: The Mackie Control Universal is a fantastic MIDI mix controller.

usually only need to adjust one thing at a time. For those who prefer the old-school approach of mixing as a discrete process, however, the ability to adjust multiple levels at once using real faders, and generally engage more physically with the mix, can be inspiring and productive.

Hot Tip

If you own a MIDI keyboard with knobs and/or faders on it, you can use those in lieu of a dedicated mix controller, although the experience may not be quite as compelling.

Three Great Mix Controllers

- **Mackie Control Universal Pro**: From one of the world's leading manufacturers of actual audio mixers comes this comprehensive controller, complete with dual displays and flying faders, and compatible with any DAW running the Mackie Control protocol – which is pretty much all of them. Add more knobs and faders with the C4 and Extender Pro expansion units. £999/$1535, **www.mackie.com**

○ **Nektar Panorama P1**: Designed to give deep control of an ever-increasing range of supported DAWs, and standard MIDI control of all others, the P1 is a solid, affordable option. £245/$376.57, **www.nektartech.com**

Above: Touch your mixes with the handsome and easy-to-use DS1.

○ **Livid Instruments DS1**: No bespoke protocols here – just good old-fashioned standard MIDI – but the DS1 is a very usable, fuss-free controller. £399/$613, **www.lividinstruments.com**

THE BASICS: BUSSING, LEVELS & PANNING

THE MIXER

The mixer is where all the audio signals in a project are brought together for balancing, processing and merging into a cohesive mix.

A QUICK TOUR OF THE MIXER

Before we delve into the specifics, let's get an overview:

1. **Level Faders:** Set the volume level for each channel in the mix, from silent to very loud indeed, with these faders.

2. **Pan Pots:** Position sounds in the stereo panorama, from fully left to fully right or anywhere in between.

3. **Mute and Solo:** Silence a channel by activating its mute button, or hear it in isolation with a click of the solo button.

4. **EQ:** While all DAWs come with their own EQ plug-ins, some display their frequency response curves directly in the mixer, while others even put the EQ controls themselves directly on each channel strip.

5. **Effects Inserts:** EQ, dynamics and distortion plug-ins, as well as all manner of creative effects, are inserted into each channel by loading them into these slots.

6. **Effects Sends:** To share an effect between multiple sounds (placing separate vocal tracks in the same virtual space via a shared reverb, for example), insert the plug-in into a return and use these controls to send the signal from each mixer channel to that effect discretely, in parallel with the channel's dry signal.

⑦ **Effects Returns**: Effects to be shared between multiple sounds are inserted into return channels (also known as auxiliary busses), where they're fed via each mix channel's send controls. The return can be adjusted like any other channel, with its own volume, pan, sends, etc.

⑧ **Group**: Most software mixers enable you to route the outputs of multiple channels to a single group or submix buss (a buss being simply a signal path to which multiple signals can be routed), for levelling, panning and processing as one combined channel.

⑨ **Master Buss**: The final destination for all the channels and busses in the mixer is the master buss, where the incoming signals are summed and processed with effects if necessary, and their overall output level adjusted.

(Not shown) Phase Reverse Switches: Some mixers also feature phase reverse switches on every channel, for correcting phase issues with multiple signals captured from the same source.

TWO APPROACHES TO MIXING

There are two approaches you can take to mixing, as described here.

The Discrete Mixdown Stage

Back in the days of analogue mixers and tape, mixing used to be tackled as a separate part of the production process to the composition and arrangement stages. Since the mixer could only be set up for one mix at a time – rather than effortlessly recalled as part of each project, as it can in software – one track needed to be finished before you could move on to the next.

Having set all the mixer controls to zero or neutral, the engineer would build the mix up one sound/group at a time. Automated mixing desks with instant recall of stored set-ups (first hardware, then software) have made this approach optional rather than unavoidable, but it is still the path preferred by many producers.

Mixing As You Go

With the software DAW's mixer set-up saved as part of its host project, the producer no longer needs to make a clear distinction between the composition, arrangement, sound design and mixing processes. Rather, mix adjustments can be made at any and every stage of production. Of course, when the track is finished, there's nothing stopping you saving a new version of the project file, zeroing the mixer and trying the alternative, discrete mixdown technique too.

Hot Tip

Whichever mixing approach you take, be sure to frequently A/B compare your mix-in-progress with a commercial track that you love the sound of, with the goal of getting it in the same sonic ballpark.

Below: Resetting the mixer and starting from zero might be old school, but it's still an effective technique.

SETTING LEVELS AND PANNING

Let's start with the basics, establishing the volume level and stereo positioning of each channel. Although our suggested order of instrumentation is only relevant to the discrete mixdown technique, the principles involved are the same for both approaches.

SETTING LEVELS

Follow our tips here and you will soon have your levels set.

Start with the Drums

There are no rules to the order in which the instrumentation in a mix should be dealt with, but it's generally a good idea to start with the drums, since they form the bedrock of most tracks.

Below: Get your drums mixed right and you're off to a great start.

If your drums comprise multiple channels (kick, snare, hi-hats, toms, cymbals, hand percussion), you'll want to group them and set up a submix, balancing their relative levels, before setting the overall level of the kit. As a starting point, with the master fader at unity (0dB), adjust the group-level fader to get your drums peaking between -6dB and -9dB.

Above: Bass can be tricky to mix due to its headroom-eating low frequencies.

Bass in the Place

Bass is possibly the trickiest sound of all when it comes to mixing, with excessive low frequencies all too easily pushing the meters into the red to no audible benefit. So, if your bass sounds puzzlingly quiet even though the meter is showing plenty of level, start by inserting a high-pass filter set to get rid of everything below a point between 40 and 80 Hz (depending on your bass sound). With that done, balancing the bass with the drums is all about feeling its interaction with the kick drum, in particular, and the overall groove in general. Adjust the bass so that the two sound like they're working together rather than drowning each other out.

Above: There's nothing more important than the vocal, so make sure it can be clearly heard.

Vocals, Guitars and Other Lead Sounds

With the drums and bass balanced, you have a solid foundation on which to build the rest of the mix. If it's a song, then the clarity of the vocal takes precedence over all else – every word should be distinctly audible at all times.

Similarly, guitars, synth leads and other primary melodic elements should be coherent and upfront, but without overwhelming the rhythm section (bass and drums). This is as much down to EQ and dynamics processing – which we'll come to later – as volume levelling, but at this stage, you want the levels set so that these kinds of sounds sit comfortably on top of everything else.

Strings and Pads

Synth pads and sustained orchestral strings playing block chords or extended series of contiguous notes can easily start to feel relentless, so they'll often need their volume levels automated or sidechain compression applied in order to prevent them from swamping the mix. Prior to that though, get any such sounds to a volume at which you think they work well, sitting behind the drums and bass, then lower the level fader a touch further. If they sound noticeably quiet once you've lived with them for a while, push them up again – it's usually better to have a pad slightly too low in the mix than slightly too high.

> ## Hot Tip
>
> **The more modulated and animated your pad sounds, the more attention-grabbing it will be. Bear this in mind when setting its volume level.**

Above: Synth pads work best in a supportive role most of the time.

Going Solo

Despite its unassuming appearance, the solo button is a mildly controversial thing. Some engineers never solo anything, figuring that if a sound is only ever meant to be part of a broader mix, what benefit can there possibly be in hearing it on its own?

However, as long as you don't become dependent on it for every mixing decision you make, there's really no reason to actively avoid those solo buttons, particularly for group channels, where hearing, say, the whole drum kit on its own in order to rebalance its component parts, is a wholly valid exercise.

None of this applies to mutes, incidentally, which should see plenty of action throughout the mixing process.

Above: The solo button is there to be used, but don't rely on it too much.

Don't Go Into the Red!

Although letting the individual channels, groups and auxiliaries in any modern DAW drift into the red occasionally won't do your mix any harm, since their (at least) 32-bit mixing engines can handle incredibly high signal levels, the outputs to your audio interface (i.e., the master output and any additional outs that you might be using to feed a hardware mixer) must never exceed 0dB. If they do, the result will be digital clipping and distortion, which is never a good thing.

As a general rule, have the master output peaking at around -3dB and, therefore, individual channels considerably lower – that's why we started with the drums tickling -6 to -9dB earlier.

Above: See all that red on the master output meter? That means it's time to turn everything down.

It's Not Over Till It's Over

Whichever of the aforementioned two approaches to mixing you take (discrete process or as-you-go), you'll inevitably find yourself returning to already-tweaked channels and rebalancing them as other parts fall into place and effects are applied. Even if you start with plenty of headroom available (as we did with our drums), it's all too easy for the master output meter to creep into the red, demanding a reassessment of the whole mix. When this happens, you can either reach for the master fader or select all the mixer channels and reduce them together by the same amount. Many engineers prefer to keep the master fader at unity (0dB), but there's no compelling technical reason to do so.

Above: Many DAWs – Logic Pro X included – let you select multiple channels and adjust their levels together.

PANNING

Charging at the pan pots like a bull at a gate can easily result in a confusing, unfocused soundstage. Here's how to get it right.

Centre of Excellence

The most important thing to bear in mind when it comes to panning is that the heart of the groove needs to remain central at all times. So that's the bass and drums, essentially. Sure, you can knock the hi-hats a bit off to one side and spread the toms and cymbals out, but keep the kick and snare straight down the middle; and no matter how chorused your bass might be, make sure the dry signal remains dead centre.

Above: The kick and snare should always be central; toms and hi-hats can be panned.

After that, vocals, lead lines, lead guitar parts and other headline sounds should also be mostly centred, with stereo width supplied by reverb and delay-based effects.

Controlling the Soundstage

With your drums, bass and lead elements panned centrally, don't fall into the trap of thinking you can then throw everything else out to the sides with wild abandon.

Hot Tip

Be mindful of whether or not your panning is making the mix feel wonky – any element that stays around for any length of time on one side or the other should be counter-balanced by a complementary or related element on the opposite sound.

While special effects and low-level background sounds can range out to the extremes, anything that you want the listener to actually take notice of in a compositional sense should stay within the middle 90–120 degrees of the 180-degree (headphones) panorama.

The Third Dimension

As well as thinking in terms of left and right panning, view your mix as a three-dimensional soundstage, in which instruments and other elements can also be moved from front to back, towards and away from the listener.

To give the impression that a part is off in the distance, apply a low-pass filter and/or diffuse reverb with the top end rolled off. Then, to really push the sound off into the background, use a delay plug-in to emulate the effect of it echoing around a large environment.

Below: Use a big, diffuse-filtered reverb to make parts sound like they're a long way away.

Only do this when you have a bright, confident front to your soundstage though – background sounds in a music mix only work when there's a foreground to give them context.

ON THE BUSSES

We've mentioned group bussing several times in this chapter – here's how it's done.

Group Bussing

1. In our Ableton Live project, we have a collection of closely related drum and percussion tracks that we'd like to bring together under the control of a single-channel fader.

2. To set up the group, we simply select all the tracks/channels to be included, right-click one and choose Group Tracks. The tracks and their mixer channels are all put into a governing group channel folder.

3. Not only do we now have one-fader control of the drum and percussion section volume, but we can also insert effects plug-ins into the group to process it. Here, we're applying Live's Glue Compressor and EQ Eight.

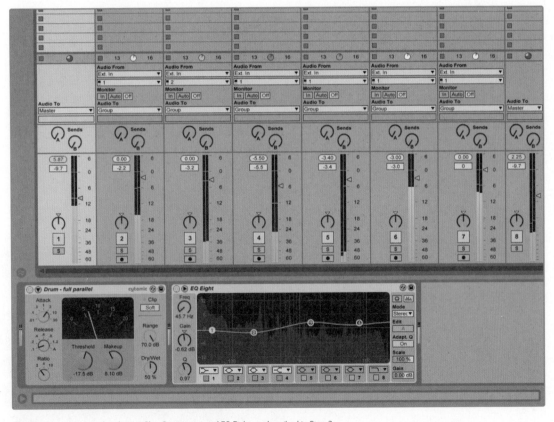

Above: Shown here are the plug-ins Glue Compressor and EQ Eight, as described in Step 3.

MID/SIDE PROCESSING

This powerful mixing technique gives you fine control over the stereo width and central impact of your sounds.

WHAT IS MID/ SIDE PROCESSING?

Using a mid/side-enabled plug-in (which could be a dedicated mid/side processor or an EQ, compressor, etc. with a mid/side mode), any stereo signal can be encoded into a mid signal, comprising all of the information common to both the left and right channels – i.e., the mono centre – and a sides signal, containing everything else – all information specific to either channel. These two signals can then be adjusted and processed separately (one in the left channel, the other in the right) before being decoded back into a regular stereo signal.

Hot Tip

If you don't have any mid/ side-enabled plug-ins in your collection, head to www.voxengo.com and take advantage of the free MSED.

Above: Voxengo MSED is an essential freebie.

WHAT CAN YOU DO WITH IT?

The most basic yet important purpose served by mid/side processing is balancing the levels of the mid and side signals – emphasizing the sides for width, or the middle for punch, for example. However, by applying EQ and/or compression to one or both signals, truly surgical reshaping of stereo sounds becomes possible, with certain plug-ins geared up to really capitalize on the concept. DMG Audio's Compassion compressor, for example, can be set up so that the side signal is compressed whenever the mid signal exceeds the threshold, or vice versa. Introduce more overtly creative effects into the equation – reverb, chorus, auto-filter, etc. – and a world of interesting, mix-enhancing possibilities opens up.

Below: Compassion can do clever things with mid/side processing.

Centering a Wide Bass Sound with MSED

1. We've got a big, chorused synth bassline that's too wide for the mix (bass should always be centre-focused, remember), but we don't want to attenuate the chorus effect because it's an integral part of the tone. Voxengo MSED gives us the answer.

Above: MSED has the ability to swap the stereo channels, among other functions.

2. We insert MSED into the channel, operating in Inline mode. This makes it encode the stereo signal to M/S format, process it with its onboard level and pan controls, then decode it back to stereo.

3. To bring in the stereo sides of our bass, we lower the Side Gain control – the chorus effect remains intact, but the whole sound becomes more centrally weighted, just as a bass should be.

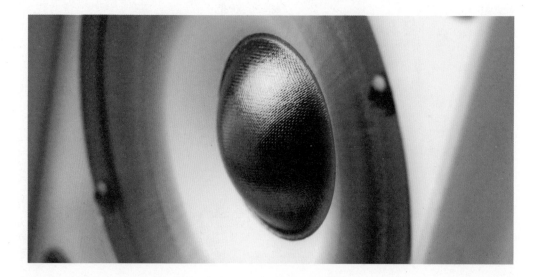

Mid/Side EQ in Action

1. Using mid/side processing, we can EQ the centre and side portions of a sound completely independently of each other. We could do this using any EQ plug-in capable of separately processing the left and right channels, preceded and followed by MSED in Encode and Decode modes respectively, but instead, we'll use FabFilter Pro-Q 2, which has mid/side functionality built in.

2. All we have to do is insert Pro-Q 2 in the channel of the sound to be processed, switch it from Stereo to Mid/Side mode, and set each EQ filter to Mid or Side to create a discrete curve for each signal. The plug-in handles the encoding and decoding for us. Nice!

Below: ProQ2 enables you to EQ the mid and side signals separately.

DYNAMICS & EQ

DYNAMICS: COMPRESSION

To get your mix sounding smooth and consistent, you need to become a dab hand at compression.

WHAT'S IT FOR?

Before the invention of the compressor, any adjustment to the level of an audio signal, no matter how short-lived, in order to keep it within a certain dynamic range, had to be made manually by the engineer. Compressor plug-ins automate the process, enabling signals that vary in volume level to be effortlessly flattened down to a narrower dynamic range.

Without compression, a mix (particularly one involving acoustic and electric instruments) can fluctuate dynamically so much that it becomes awkward and odd to listen to. Compression not only makes a track sound more professional, but can also be used to shape individual parts and/or the whole mix, making them sound more punchy, weighty and exciting.

Right: Compression is one of the most important mixing techniques to master.

HOW DOES IT WORK?

Here, you will learn what the main controls on your compressor plug-in do.

Threshold and Ratio

The two most important controls on any compressor are Threshold and Ratio. Threshold sets the input volume level at which the compressor starts to do its thing, while Ratio determines how much compression is applied.

Threshold is the easiest of the two to get a handle on: the compressor does nothing to the signal until it reaches the set Threshold; when the Threshold is exceeded, compression is applied; when the signal drops below the Threshold again, compression stops being applied. Easy.

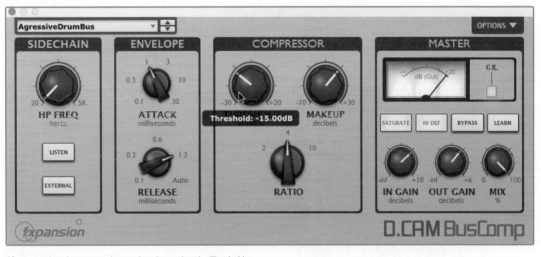

Above: Nothing happens to the signal until it reaches the Threshold.

Ratio is a little less straightforward. When the signal exceeds the Threshold, the amount of compression applied is set by the Ratio, which reduces the amount of gain by a fixed amount, expressed as ... well, a ratio.

Let's say we have a wildly fluctuating drum track that peaks at -5dB, with a compressor plugin inserted into its mixer channel set to -15dB Threshold (i.e., compressing the signal whenever it exceeds -15dB). With the Ratio set to 5:1, for every 5dB by which the drums exceed -15dB, the signal at the compressor output will only rise by 1dB. So, whenever the drums hit -5dB prior to the compressor, the compressor reduces (compresses) the level to -13dB (-15+ (10/5)=-13). If the Ratio was 2:1, -5dB at input would become -10dB at output.

Below: The Ratio setting controls how much compression is applied.

Attack and Release

A compressor's Attack and Release parameters specify how long the gain reduction (compression) takes to kick in and withdraw respectively, when the input signal exceeds then drops back below the Threshold.

Continuing our drums example, if you compress the whole signal immediately the Threshold is passed, you'll also reduce the volume of the all-important kick/snare attack transients, which is not usually desirable. To get round this, increase the Attack so that compression is applied after a few milliseconds, allowing the crack of each hit to be retained.

Now imagine a bass part, playing sustained notes. With the Release set too fast, the compressor won't catch the sustain portion; by lengthening it, you can control exactly how much of the signal is attenuated before the compression backs off.

> ## Hot Tip
>
> **Many compressors feature an Auto Release setting, which automatically adjusts the Release according to the material being compressed.**

Below: Tailor your compressor's response with the Attack and Release controls.

Knee

The abruptness of the transition from no compression to and from full compression is set by the Knee control. By default, most compressors jump to full compression almost immediately (a hard Knee) when the signal passes the Threshold, but by softening the Knee, the transition can be made more gradual, starting just before the Threshold, for a smoother gain reduction onset.

Above: FabFilter's Pro-C offers Hard and Soft Knee settings, and Auto Gain.

Make-up Gain

Compression reduces the difference between the loudest and quietest parts of a signal by lowering the former, thus the overall level at the output of the compressor is lower than that at the input. The Make-up Gain control brings it back up. Many compressors also offer an automatic make-up setting, which matches the average output level to the input level.

Mix

The compressor's Mix control lets you set a balance between the processed (wet) and unprocessed (dry) output of the compressor. For a fully compressed signal, it should be set at 100 per cent wet; but by blending some dry signal in with the wet, you can combine the natural dynamics of the uncompressed source with the punch and weight of the (high-Ratio) compressed signal. This technique is called parallel or New York compression (due to its popularity with studio engineers in the Big Apple some years ago), and it can be particularly effective on acoustic drums. Not all compressors feature Mix controls, but you can still achieve parallel compression with those that don't by running them on an auxiliary return.

Above: Native Instruments Vari Comp compressor features a Dry level control rather than a Mix knob, but the end result is the same.

COMPRESSION IN ACTION

Now let's get down to business, applying compression to a variety of sources.

Compressing a Drum Kit

1. As well as on individual instruments, compressors are also often deployed on group busses, such as that of a drum kit, comprising the combined outputs of its component tracks (kick, snare, hi-hats, etc.).

2. Ableton Live's Glue Compressor is an excellent choice for drums. Here, we're using it on a kick/hi-hats/clap buss. We start by setting the Threshold to compress a good portion of the signal (not just the extreme peaks), then dial in a 4:1 Ratio.

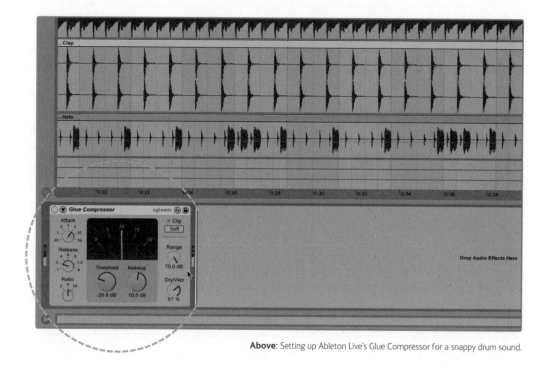

Above: Setting up Ableton Live's Glue Compressor for a snappy drum sound.

3. Setting the Attack to 3 ms and Release to 200 ms gives us a good combination of transient snap, kick drum sustain and breathing space. Bringing back some dry signal with the Mix control adds a touch of dynamic movement, and raising the Make-up Gain brings the overall level back up.

Compressing Bass Guitar

1. Compressing bass is all about the Attack and Release. Start by setting the Threshold to catch the peaks in the signal and the Ratio somewhere between 2:1 and 4:1.

2. How much Attack transient should be let through via adjustment of the Attack control will depend on the type of sound you're after – lengthen it until you get a pleasing amount of pluck.

3. Similarly, adjust the Release to achieve compression of as much of the sustain tail as befits the part. Auto Release can be effective, here.

> ## Hot Tip
>
> **Synth bass is more amenable to higher Ratios and experimentation with Attack and Release settings than bass guitar, which the ear generally expects to sound a certain way.**

Above: Bringing up the sustain of a bass using compressor Release.

Compressing Electric Guitar

1. How much compression any given electric guitar part requires will depend in large part on whether or not it's been recorded clean or through an overdriven amp. If a lot of overdrive has been applied, then you might only need a touch of compression – if any – since overdrive levels the signal on its own.

2. When compression is called for, however (when you're dealing with a cleaner type of sound), it should be approached in a similar way to how it is with bass: Ratio up to around 4:1 or 5:1; enough Attack to let the note definition through; enough Release to give the sustain presence.

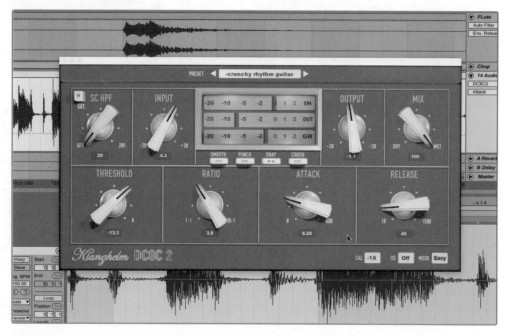

Above: If your electric guitar needs any compression at all, approach it as you would electric bass.

Compressing Acoustic Guitar

1. Tread very carefully when compressing acoustic guitar, as it's all too easy to suck the life out of what should be a sensitive, dynamic instrument. Indeed, be absolutely sure that your guitar needs compressing at all – it might not, particularly if it's solo or accompanied only by a vocal.

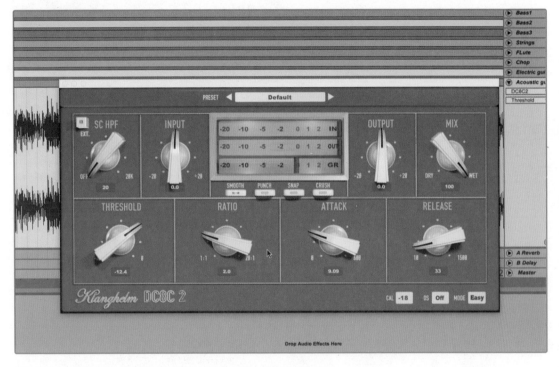

Above: Gentle compression should be all that's needed – if anything – for acoustic guitar.

2. If you do decide to compress your acoustic, the settings will depend on the playing style (strummed or picked), but generally speaking, set the Threshold so that only the peaks are brought down, and keep the Ratio low – 2:1 will often be sufficient. Attack should be moderately fast (15–30 ms), while Release should be appropriate to the style and tempo of the track, but probably quite fast. Try a soft Knee setting too.

Compressing Vocals

1. Even more so than acoustic guitar, vocals should be handled with great care when it comes to compression (or any other process). Being the centrepiece of the song, it's absolutely imperative that they sound natural, clear and present at all times, much of which is down to their dynamic shaping.

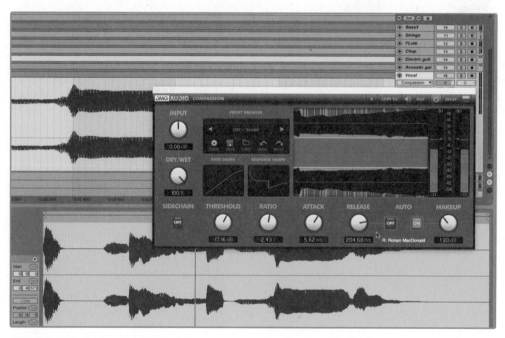

Above: Take great care when compressing vocals.

2. Low Ratios and carefully positioned Thresholds (a choice determined largely by the quality of the vocal performance and the genre of the track) are the order of the day. Attack times should be short, while Release can extend into the hundreds of milliseconds, depending on the vibe and how much breath you want to bring out.

Sidechain Compression

Most compressor plug-ins these days feature a sidechain input, enabling the compression to be triggered in response to an external signal (known as the key) instead of the main input – the compressor acts as if it's processing the key input, but is actually applied to the main input.

Sidechain compression is incredibly useful when you want one element of the mix to lower (or duck) the volume of another element. Examples include dropping the volume of the bass whenever the kick drum hits to avoid low-end clashes, and bringing a vocal to the forefront by (very gently!) ducking the rest of the mix whenever it's present.

> ## Hot Tip
>
> A popular technique in four-to-the-floor dance music is to run a compressor on the master output, with its sidechain input keyed off the kick drum for a global pumping effect.

Above: Sidechain compression is a ubiquitous technique in all styles of music production.

De-essing

Although there are plenty of plug-ins dedicated to reducing sibilant sounds ('s' and 'sh') in vocals, you can make your own de-esser using a sidechain-equipped compressor and an EQ.

Insert a compressor into your vocal channel, feed a copy of the vocal into its sidechain input and EQ it to heavily emphasize the sibilant frequencies. Set the Threshold so that the compressor only reacts to those peaks and the volume of the vocal will be reduced whenever sibilance occurs. Use a fast Attack and Release, and a Ratio that lowers the sibilance to a point that still sounds natural.

Some compressors have filters or EQ built into their internal sidechain circuits, enabling the same process to be applied entirely internally, without the need for a duplicate signal.

Below: Live's built-in Compressor lets you EQ its internal sidechain for easy de-essing.

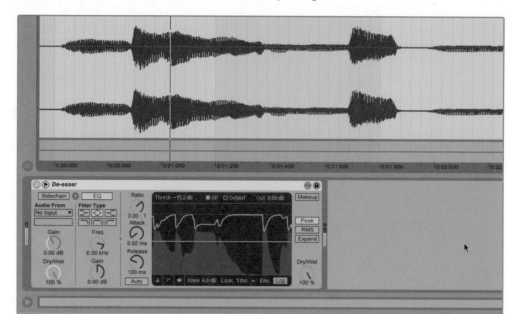

DYNAMICS: LIMITING

Whether you want to volunteer for the loudness war or just use all available headroom without danger of clipping, limiting is your friend.

WHAT'S IT FOR?

Limiting is simply compression at a very high Ratio (from 10:1 up to infinity:1). While you can use most compressors for limiting, there are many dedicated limiter plug-ins available that are tuned specifically to the purpose.

Like compression, limiting is used to increase perceived loudness. Although you can just set a limiter up to rein in troublesome peaks and prevent clipping on the master output (peaks exceeding 0dB) without noticeably affecting the overall signal, they're also employed for more overt dynamic shaping. The oft-discussed loudness war of modern music production is largely a result of the excessive use of brick-wall limiting at the mastering stage in order to crush the dynamic range of pop and dance tracks.

Above: FabFilter's Pro-L limiter more than lives up to its name.

HOW DOES IT WORK?

Limiting is a simpler concept to get your head round than compression, but you still need to understand a few key controls.

Ceiling or Output Level

The first thing to decide when setting up a limiter is what level, in decibels, its output should be limited to (you can't adjust the Ratio on a limiter – it's fixed at a very high setting, usually infinity:1). Set the Ceiling or Output Level (different plug-ins use different names) to -0.1dB, for example, and the output of the limiter will never exceed -0.1dB.

Below: Set the upper limit of your limiter output with the Ceiling control.

Well, almost never: inter-sample peaks in a digital audio signal can slip past limiters not designed to deal with them, causing clipping. For that reason, it's a good idea to set the Ceiling on such plug-ins lower than the standard 0dB; -0.6dB should alleviate any potential problems.

Input Gain

Following on from the Output Level Ceiling concept, a limiter's Input Gain setting is analogous to the height of the floor. It determines how hard the incoming signal is driven into the limiter (raising the floor as it's increased), and thus how squashed it becomes as it pushes up against the Ceiling. With the Input Gain pushed to extremes, the dynamic range can be reduced to almost nothing, resulting in an extremely aggressive, distorted signal that will be perceived as louder than it actually is, even if it doesn't sound terribly nice.

Setting the Input Gain correctly can make the difference between a punchy, energetic, lively mix and a loud, crunchy, but ultimately lifeless one.

Below: Set your Input Gain too high and horrible distortion will be your reward.

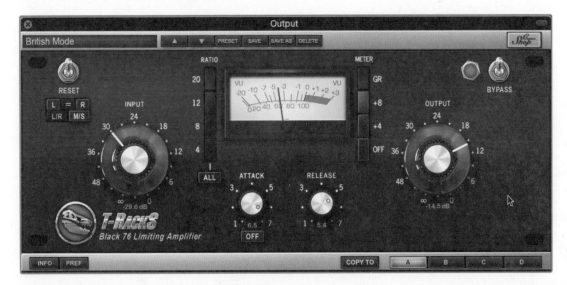

Release

Since limiters are intended primarily to respond quickly and transparently to Attack transients, it should come as no surprise that their Release settings are generally kept pretty fast. Most limiter plug-ins will offer Release speeds down to 0.1 ms, although some will go as fast as 0.01 ms or even 0 ms; and up to a second or more. The majority of the time, you'll want to stay at the lower end of this range, with the timing set precisely to suit the shape and tempo of the track. Longer settings can be useful for characterful pumping effects.

Above: Limiter Release should take its cue from the transients of the track – you'll usually want it to be fast.

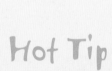

Hot Tip

Most limiter plug-ins don't have Attack controls, since the onset of limiting is almost always required to be as fast as possible.

Lookahead

Time and physics being what they are, a hardware limiter in the real world can never achieve perfect brick-wall limiting, since it can't see into the future to start clamping down on fast transients before they actually occur.

Software limiter plug-ins, however, can, thanks to the Lookahead parameter, which can be set to 'look ahead' an adjustable number of milliseconds and see transients before they arrive, and start its Attack accordingly for true brick walling.

The downside to this otherwise miraculous feature is increased latency, which shouldn't be an issue at the mixing stage, depending on how well your DAW handles it.

Above: See into the future with your limiter's Lookahead function.

DYNAMICS: GATING

The last dynamics processor on our list is the gate: use it to do away with background noise and tighten up instrumental elements.

WHAT'S IT FOR?

The gate (or noise gate, to give it its full name) is closely related to the compressor, in that both are designed to lower the level of the input signal. However, while the compressor does it when the signal exceeds a user-specified Threshold, the gate does it when the signal drops below the Threshold. Although the amount of attenuation applied by the gate can usually be adjusted, the default is reduction to silence.

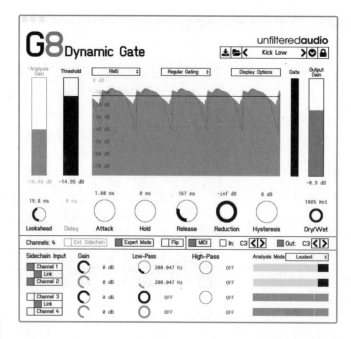

So, by setting the Threshold slightly higher than the level of background noise in a recording, the signal only passes through the gate to be heard when it rises above that level – i.e., when the recorded instrument is playing.

Beside its noise-eliminating role, creative uses for gates include tightening up drums, basses and other transient-heavy parts, and rhythmically chopping sustained sounds.

Left: Unfiltered Audio's G8 Gate is one of the most feature-packed gates around.

HOW DO YOU USE IT?

Your gate will feature a number of standard controls and parameters. Here's how they work.

Threshold

The inverse of its compressor counterpart, the gate's Threshold marks the volume level that the input signal has to exceed to be heard at the output. When the signal falls below the Threshold, it's gated out and silenced (or attenuated by a user-specified amount using the Range control). Chattering around the Threshold can be countered using the Hysteresis control (see page 72).

Range/Reduction/ Attenuation/Floor

Many names for the same control, which specifies the amount of volume reduction applied when the signal falls below the Threshold. Much of the time, this will be set to -infinity dB, for gating to total silence, but there will be times when you want to merely reduce the level of a sound rather than kill it altogether.

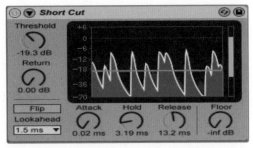

Above: Ableton Live's Gate set to completely gate out everything below -19.3 dB.

Envelope

Most gates feature three adjustable envelope stages: Attack, Hold and Release. Attack sets the time it takes for the gate to open fully when the input signal exceeds the Threshold – use it to smooth the transition from silence to audibility. Hold then establishes the length of time that the gate remains open when the signal drops

Above: PSP Audioware's MixGate uses virtual LEDs to visualize the action of the gate, rather than a graphical display.

back below the Threshold, while Release is the time it takes for the gate to close again once the Hold stage has completed – use these two to tailor the gate to reverb tails, sustained sounds, etc.

Hysteresis

Input signal fluctuations around the Threshold level can cause the gate to open and close rapidly (chattering). The Hysteresis control sets a second Threshold a user-specified number of decibels below the main one: the gate opens when the higher Threshold is exceeded and closes when the lower one is undershot, creating breathing space between them.

Sidechain and EQ

Most gates feature an external sidechain input, via which their action can be triggered by a separate keying signal for creative purposes – imposing the rhythmic shape of a drum loop on to a synth pad, say.

Above: Use the Hysteresis control to eliminate chatter.

You might also find EQ controls on your gate plug-in. Rather than processing the audible output, these work on the internal sidechain to prevent the gate from responding to specific frequencies.

EQUALIZATION

Let's now turn our attention to the frequency content of the mix and the EQ plug-ins that are used to reshape it.

WHAT'S IT FOR?

While compression is used to shape the volume of a signal, equalization is used to alter its frequency content. Applying EQ is such an essential part of the mixing process that you'll find yourself doing it to the vast majority of sounds in all your mixes.

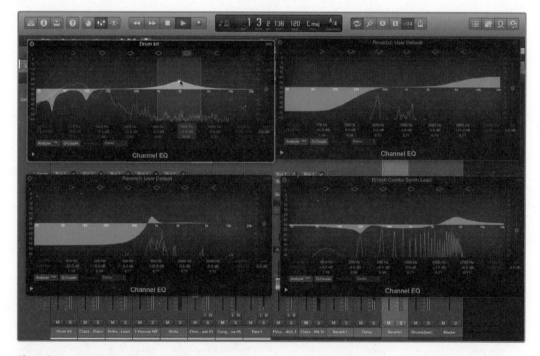

Above: Becoming an expert at EQ is essential, because you're going to be using an awful lot of it.

EQ gives you the means by which to prevent sounds clashing and brings clarity, air and balance to the mix. By cutting away unnecessary frequencies and/or boosting essential ones, clutter is reduced and the essence of each part is brought into focus. When EQ is employed tastefully and with care, the results can be truly magnificent.

EQ TYPES

There are a huge variety of EQ plug-ins on the market, from emulations of classic analogue hardware units to ultra-precise, multi-mode modules and everything in between. No matter what their functional and sonic differences though, they all draw on three core filter types: low-/high-pass, shelving and bell or peaking.

Low/High-pass Filters

Many EQs include low- and high-pass (often called high- and low-cut) filters for cutting off everything above or below their specified frequencies. These filters might also offer Resonance controls for emphasizing the cut-off points, and a choice of roll-off slopes; although many won't let you adjust anything more than the Cutoff frequency, requiring a dedicated filter to be deployed if more detailed high/low filtering is required.

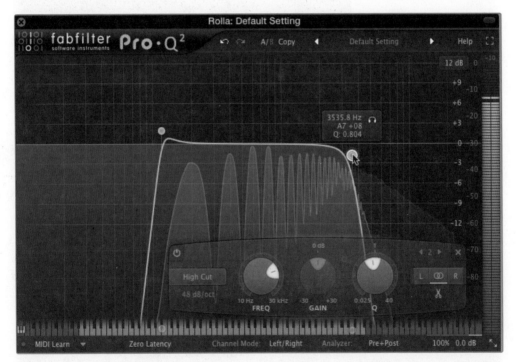

Above: Low- and high-pass EQ filters.

Shelving EQ

The shelving EQ filter cuts or boosts all frequencies above (high shelf) or below (low shelf) the dialled-in frequency. When you need to lift or lower the bass or treble sections of a sound in a broad-strokes fashion, the shelves should be your first port of call.

Bell/Peaking EQ

With high-/low-pass and shelving filters being ideal for making big changes to the top and bottom ends of a sound, everything in the middle is handled using one or more bell or peaking filters, which are typically of a parametric design.

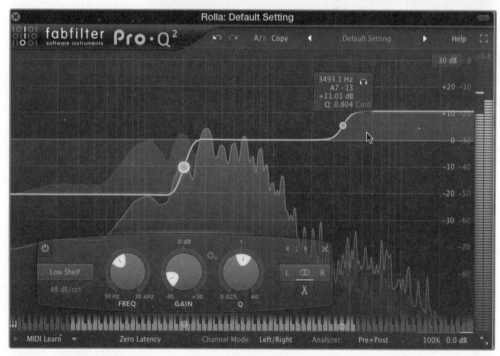

Above: A low shelf attenuating from 200Hz down, and a high shelf boosting above 3.5 kHz.

The name 'bell' comes from the bell-shaped response curve of the filter, and 'parametric' means that a trio of adjustable parameters are used to manipulate it: Frequency, Gain and Q. Frequency is the centre frequency of the curve; Gain is the amount by which the peak of the curve is boosted or attenuated in decibels; and Q is the width of the curve. Between them, these three controls enable sculpting of signals using everything from broadband scoops to surgical incisions.

Hot Tip

The graphic EQ consists of a number (from three to 30+) of fixed-frequency band-pass filters, spaced out at regular intervals across the audible frequency range. Due to its lack of precision, graphic EQ is of limited use at the mixing stage.

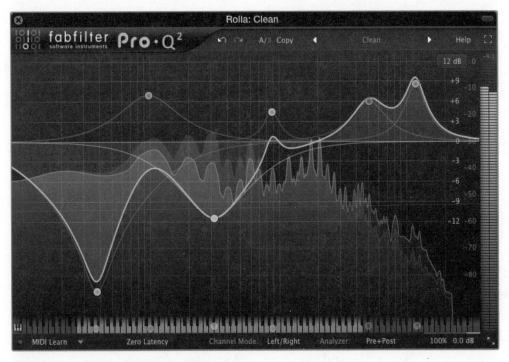

Above: Six parametric EQ bands shaping a complex response curve.

Vintage vs Modern EQ

Although you might assume that the latest high-precision EQ plug-ins would outclass less flexible vintage emulations in all areas and should therefore always be your first choice, there are two very good reasons why that's not actually the case:

1. Virtual revivals of classic models by the likes of Pultec, API and Neve sporting comparatively limited controls can be easy to use next to their more powerful contemporary descendants.

2. The sound. Most modern EQs are designed to be totally transparent, but many classic analogue units are sought-after for the specific tonal colouration and warmth that their amplification circuitry introduces to the signal, and that's often replicated in software emulations of them.

Above: IK Multimedia's Neve and API EQ emulations sound incredible.

ESSENTIAL EQ TECHNIQUES

EQ is a multipurpose tool. Here are the main tasks you'll find yourself using it for.

Clearing Space

The primary role of EQ is cutting away frequencies that just don't need to be present in every sound in the mix, in order to give all of them as much space as possible. Examples include thinning out guitars to make room

Above: Notching the muddy low-mid frequencies out of a bassline.

for vocals, or cutting notches in the bass to reduce mud and honk. For wide, sweeping cuts, use your EQ's high-/low-pass filters and shelves; for more targeted sculpting, reach for those parametric peaking bands.

Since over-accumulation of low frequencies is a sure-fire way to ruin any mix, it's usually a good idea to high-pass filter every individual channel, getting rid of unnecessary (and unheard), headroom-devouring bottom end. Raise the Cutoff frequency on each track's filter until it actually starts to have a noticeable effect on the sound, then back it off slightly. Although you won't hear it make much, if any, difference to each sound when you listen to them in isolation, the effect on the mix when it all comes together will be significant – tighter bass, less low-mid clutter and increased headroom across the board.

Above: High-pass filtering every track in the mix for a tight, punchy low end.

This applies to bass sounds too: depending on the genre you're in, even the lowest of sub-basses shouldn't go below 40 Hz for dance music, while regular bass sounds should be cut at 60–80 Hz.

Enhancing Sounds

While clearing space in one sound to make room in the mix for others is done using reductive EQ cuts, emphasizing the defining characteristics of a sound usually involves boosts. Bringing out the sub element of a bass or kick drum, for example, might entail a few decibels of gain around 60 Hz.

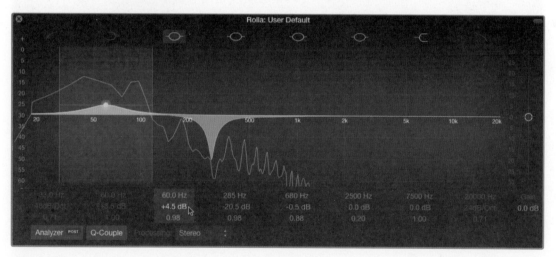

Above: Bringing up the sub element of a bassline with a broad boost centred on 60 Hz.

While cuts will often require high Q values for precision and accuracy, boosts will usually want to be quite broad. And be very careful not to push them too high: if you find yourself boosting the core frequencies of a sound by 15dB, say, it might be better to raise the level of the whole part and filter out the bits you don't want to hear.

Master Buss EQ

If you need to make sweeping frequency changes to the whole mix at any point in the mixing process, rather than going in and adjust all your channel EQs individually, don't be shy about EQing the master output.

You'll want to use your highest-quality plug-in for this – go with a linear phase mode (*see* page 118) for maximum transparency – and be extremely conservative with your cuts and boosts, particularly the latter.

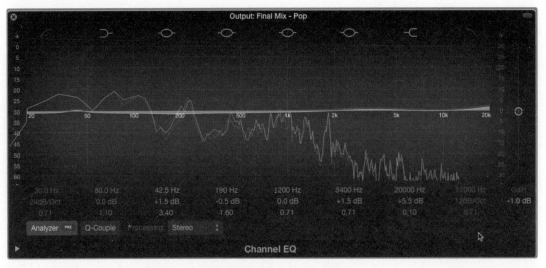

Above: Here, we're very gently EQing the master output to tighten up the whole mix.

Master buss EQ might seem like a drastic measure, but if it sounds right, it is right. If you're in any doubt at all as to its effectiveness once applied, err on the side of caution and turn it off.

Incidentally, linear phase EQ is also often the best option when multiple signals from a single source are grouped on a buss – a multi-miked drum kit, for example.

Automating EQ

Automating volume levels as a track progresses is standard mixing practice, focusing the listener's attention on the vocal in the verse and chorus, the guitar in the guitar solo, etc. However, sometimes, automating EQ instead can be more effective.

For example, rather than simply dropping the level of a guitar to make room for a vocal, then bringing it back up afterwards, try attenuating the frequencies occupied by the vocal in the guitar part via automation. The goal in this example would be to retain weight in the guitar without compromising the clarity of the vocal.

Hot Tip

Keep your EQ automation moves as gentle as possible so as not to completely change the character of the sound – unless that's your intention, of course.

Above: Automating EQ on a keyboard part to give the vocal space.

THE SWEET SPOTS

Here's a rough summary of the main frequency ranges you'll find yourself dealing with in your mixing adventures and what you can expect to achieve by cutting and boosting them. These are just guidelines, of course; precise frequencies and results will depend on your particular instrumentation and mixing style.

Key Frequencies and How to Handle Them

- **30–40 Hz:** Cut to reduce rumble.

- **40–75 Hz:** Boost to enhance sub-bass and kick-drum fundamentals, and add weight to the mix; cut to reduce boom.

- **80–200 Hz:** Boost to add body to snares and guitars, punch to kick drums, roundness to bass, and general warmth; cut to reduce low mud.

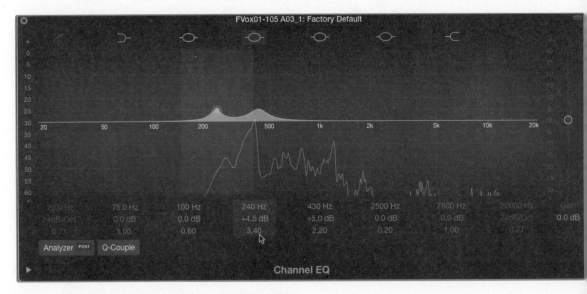

Above: Adding presence to a vocal with boosts at 240 and 430 Hz.

- **200–500 Hz**: Boost to add weight and girth to lead instruments and vocals, and presence to basses; cut to reduce mud and boxiness.

- **500–1500 Hz**: Boost to enhance drums, bass, guitars, synths, piano (and other keyboards) and vocals; cut to reduce honk and guitar scratchiness.

- **2–5 kHz**: Boost to add high-frequency definition to bass, presence to synth pads and strings, and impact to vocals; cut to reduce harshness in many instruments and vocal shrillness.

- **6–10 kHz**: Boost to add crack to kick and snare, sheen to cymbals and brightness to guitars; cut to reduce vocal sibilance.

- **15 kHz+**: Boost (with a shelving EQ) to add air and brightness to just about anything but bass and kick drums; cut to reduce fizz.

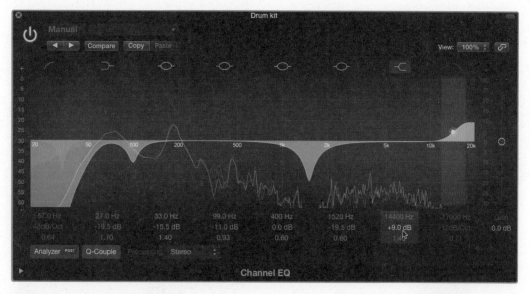

Above: Adding air to the drums with a high shelf.

MIXING EFFECTS

MIX PROCESSING FUNDAMENTALS

By applying effects plug-ins tastefully to the component tracks and busses of your mix, you can make it sound larger than life.

INSERTS AND SENDS

Effects can be directly inserted into individual channels or shared by multiple channels at once on a send/return buss.

Above: In Logic, insert effects are loaded in the Audio FX area of the mixer.

Insert Effects

These are effects that are inserted directly into a mixer channel to process just the signal on that channel. Generally speaking, insert effects include things like EQ, compression, distortion, filtering and anything else intended to be applied 100 per cent wet to just one signal. However, you can balance the mix between processed and unprocessed signal using the plug-in's wet/dry mix control, and there's no reason reverbs, delays or any other plug-ins can't also be inserted if your system resources allow it.

Auxiliary Effects

These are the plug-ins inserted into auxiliary return channels (the nomenclature varies from DAW to DAW, but they'll probably be called Aux, Return, FX channels), to which every other mixer channel can send its signal by a variable amount for processing. That amount is determined by the Send controls on each channel, and the point at which the signal is tapped for sending can be set before or after the channel's level fader. Because the

Above: Logic names its auxiliary returns 'Aux' — we've got three of them in this project.

level of signal into the plug-in is set separately for each sending channel, and the regular dry signal remains unaffected on the main channel outputs, auxiliary effects should always be set 100 per cent wet.

The main benefit of send effects is that applying, say, one reverb to five sounds uses far less CPU overhead than applying five reverbs to one sound each. For example, say you have a reverb (100 per cent wet) on your Return 1 channel. By turning up the Send 1 knobs on your drum, guitar and percussion tracks, all three are sent to the reverb at a volume level set by said knobs. At the same time, the original tracks are still audible in the mix – the Send knobs have no bearing on their outputs. The result is the same three tracks as before, but accompanied by a fully reverb-processed blend of all three (using a single plug-in!), the volume of which back in the mix is set using Return 1's level fader.

Above: Every channel with its Bus 1 send knob raised is going through this reverb.

Mix Automation

We touched on automation in Chapter 3, in reference to levels and EQ, and it's an equally important consideration when it comes to mix effects too.

Above: Automation is the key to getting your mixes moving.

Whether you're blasting the level of a send on every 32nd snare hit to drench it in reverb, or ramping up the distortion on a guitar for the chorus, your DAW's automation system should see a lot of action throughout the mixing process. And don't be afraid to be experimental with your creative effects animations – that's what undo/redo is for.

Hot Tip

Rather than draw all your automation moves in perfectly with the mouse, use a MIDI controller to record them live. That human touch could prove significant in the final mix.

ESSENTIAL EFFECTS

Your plug-ins folder is bursting with incredible devices with which to enhance, reshape and mangle your sounds. Let's take a look at the most useful from a mixing perspective.

DYNAMICS AND EQ: WHICH COMES FIRST?

We've covered compression and EQ elsewhere, but let's take a moment to consider the age-old question: which of the two should come first in the effects chain?

Above: Compressor or EQ first? It depends.

Unsurprisingly, there's no clear answer, but applying EQ to a signal will have more of a dramatic effect on a subsequent compressor than vice versa, so most of the time you'll probably want to compress first. However, that fact can also make pre-compression EQ a powerful corrective process when your compressor is being overly impacted by unrequired frequencies. Indeed, you might even need to sandwich one with two instances of the other at times.

DISTORTION: WARM IT UP

Distortion's an essential tool not just for shaping guitar tones, but also for adding bite, edge and presence to drums, bass, synths, vocals and anything else – some engineers use it almost as often as EQ and compression. There are very few sounds that aren't improved by a touch of valve saturation; while heavier overdrive and wave-shaping can be godsends for bringing energy to flaccid parts.

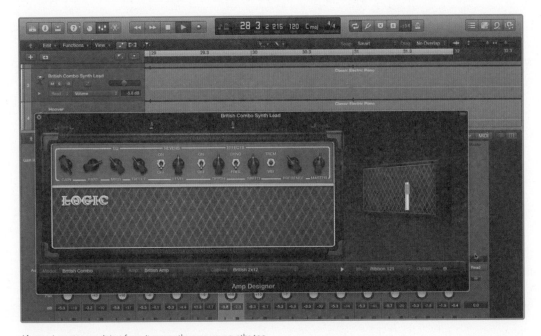

Above: Amp sims aren't just for guitars: use them on your synths too.

On a related tip, guitar amp simulations such as Native Instruments Guitar Rig and IK Multimedia Amplitube don't have to be used on guitars. Lead and bass synth sounds in particular can be utterly transformed by being blasted through a virtual amp/cab combo at the start of the effects chain.

REVERB: VIRTUAL SPACES

After compression and EQ, reverb is the most important effect in the mix engineer's arsenal, letting you position your sounds in just about any virtual space you can imagine.

Whether to plump for an algorithmic or convolution (sampled-based) reverb for any given sound will depend on how realistic you want the effect to be. To keep acoustic instruments and vocals sounding as natural as possible, convolution is the way to go; for synths, drum machines and electronic music in general, algorithmic should probably be your first choice.

Above: Convolution (left) and algorithmic (right) reverb plug-ins.

For pop and rock instrumentation, the decision might be less clear-cut, but in very broad terms, think of algorithmic as more upfront and hyped than convolution.

Gated Reverb

1. For that quintessentially 1980s Phil Collins gated reverb snare drum sound, start by inserting a reverb plug-in (100 per cent wet) into an auxiliary Return channel, followed by a gate plug-in.

2. Set the reverb to a large room preset and send the snare drum to it by raising its Send knob.

> ### Hot Tip
>
> **If your gate has an external sidechain input, key it off the snare channel so that the snare itself opens the gate, rather than the reverb.**

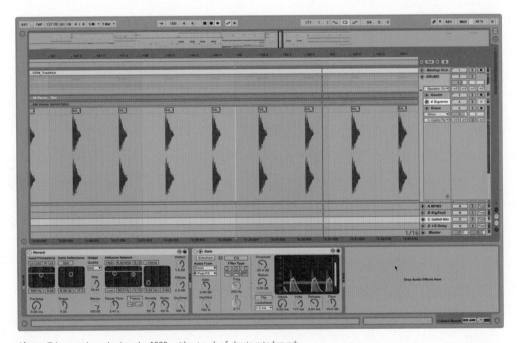

Above: Take your drums back to the 1980s with a touch of classic gated reverb.

3. Set the gate's Threshold and Hysteresis so that it opens cleanly and closes at a suitable point in the reverb decay. The Attack should be as fast as possible, the Release short, and the Hold however long you want the reverb to last.

Reverse Reverb

1. Creating the ghostly reverse reverb vocal effect heard in countless tracks of the last few decades is easy thanks to the power of the modern DAW. Start by inserting a reverb on the channel of the vocal clip to be processed.

2. Set the reverb to a large space with a decay of a few seconds, 50 per cent wet (or to taste), then reverse the vocal audio and bounce the processed track. Be sure to set the locators so that the reverb tail is rendered in full.

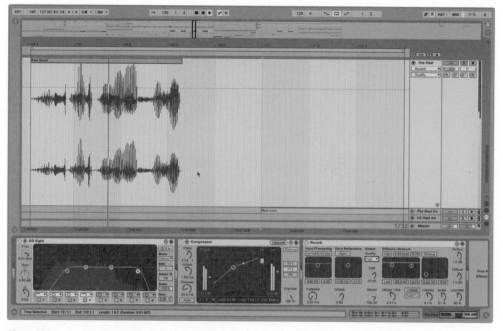

Above: Make sure you capture the full reverb tail when bouncing.

3. Mute or delete the original vocal track, then import the bounced audio file on to a new track and reverse it, flipping the reverb into reverse and the vocal back the right way round. Spooky!

DELAY: ALL ABOUT THE ECHOES

Usually deployed on an auxiliary buss, delay works by literally delaying the input signal before passing it to the output, resulting in one or more echoes, or taps, in engineering parlance. There are various types of delay plug-in available, including tape delay (for dubby, degrading feedback loops, among other things), ping-pong delay (for bouncing signals between the left and right channels), and multitap delay (for designing irregular rhythmic patterns of eight or more taps).

Above: Two very powerful delay plugins: u-he Satin and MeldaProduction MMultiBandDelay.

Delays are used in the mix for all manner of things, from placing sounds in space (very short delay can be used in lieu of a small room reverb), to phasing, flanging and chorus (all are delay-based, *see* pages 99–100), to special effects.

Using Delay

1. Let's use an automated analogue delay to build a rhythm guitar up into a dubby wash of feedback. Start by inserting an analogue delay plug-in into the guitar channel, about 50 per cent wet – we're using Audio Damage DubStation.

2. It's up to you whether or not to sync the delay to the project tempo – we're leaving ours unsynced for a looser feel. Keep the Feedback (called Regen in DubStation) low.

Below: Audio Damage's DubStation is a monster when it comes to feedback delay effects.

3. From the point in the track where you want the delay to start feeding back, automate the Feedback and Mix controls to rise; then, at the end, to fall for as long as feels appropriate. Remember to reset your automated parameters if the guitar is coming back in again later.

MODULATION EFFECTS

Our next three effects use LFO modulation of various parameters to do their respective things.

Chorus

When you need a quick and easy way to thicken up a bass, guitar, keyboard, vocal or other sound, fire up a chorus plug-in.

Below: Chorus uses modulated delay lines to enrich a sound.

Chorus works by generating one or more copies of the input signal, each delayed by 20–50 ms or so. The copies are mixed with the source sound, but have their delay times modulated by an LFO at an adjustable rate, giving the impression of multiple instruments playing together, complete with tuning variations.

Hot Tip

The main things that separate chorus from phasing and flanging are the longer delay times and the number of duplicate voices generated.

Flanging

The flanger delays a single copy of the input signal by an LFO-modulated amount and mixes it back in with the source. Unlike chorus, the delay times are very short (less than 20 ms), and feedback can be dialled in. The result is a shifting series of harmonic peaks and notches (comb filtering) that's often described as being like the sound of a jet aeroplane passing overhead.

Phasing

Phasing is very similar to flanging, in that a copy of the input is mixed back in with the source, but rather than being delayed, the phase of the copy is shifted using a series of all-pass filters, leading to variable frequency cancellation as the centre frequency is modulated by an LFO. The resultant sweeping effect is less heavy-handed than flanging.

Below: Phasing and flanging: two peas in a modulating pod.

OTHER EFFECTS

That's the cornerstone mixing effects covered, but
there are others that you'll want to investigate too.

1. **Bitcrushing and Sample Rate Reduction**:
   Toughen up feeble sounds with a bit of digital
   distortion. Don't drop too low though, unless
   you're going for chiptune sounds!

2. **Vocoding**: The famous 'robot voice'
   effect isn't just for vocals – it can be
   employed to great effect on drums and
   synths too.

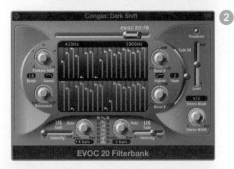

3. **Pitch and Frequency Shifting**:
   The difference between pitch and
   frequency shifter plug-ins is that
   the first retains the harmonic
   relationships between its components,
   while the second shifts the frequency
   spectrum linearly with no regard for
   such relationships. Each has its own
   sound and uses.

4. **Exciting/Enhancing**: Exciters or enhancers generate
   harmonics at specific frequencies in order to bring sheen,
   clarity and presence to the source signal. There are different
   exciters available for bass and treble enhancement duties.

Right: Some of Logic Pro's in-built effects.

MIXING TIPS & TRICKS

MIXING TIPS & TRICKS

Keep your mixing sessions on track with these big picture pointers.

REST YOUR EARS

If you've been mixing for more than an hour at any sort of volume level, your ears will be tired and you should stop for a while. We'd recommend giving it ten minutes at least. We'd also suggest not mixing for more than five or six hours a day, for the same reason.

Below: Don't lose your sonic perspective – rest your ears!

The main thing that happens when your ears start flagging is that your high-frequency hearing dulls without you realizing it, which usually results in compensatory EQ boosts that subsequently need undoing when you come back to the mix with fresh ears.

LESS IS MORE

It really is, 99 per cent of the time. Just because your DAW and plug-in effects give you more than enough processing power to effortlessly make every sound in the mix a spectacular aural tour de force in its own right, that doesn't mean you should.

The best mixes put clarity, balance and – much of the time – simplicity at the very top of the agenda. No matter the genre, in a well-mixed track, the listener's attention should be drawn to the key element (or very few elements) of your executive choosing at any given moment, with everything else supporting it (them). Automation is a powerful tool in this department, so expect to use a lot of it.

Right: What your mix doesn't say is as important as what it does.

LOUDER DOESN'T NECESSARILY MEAN BETTER

Over the last few decades, the perceived volume level of the average commercial release has crept up to an impressive but ear-splitting level in order to keep it competitive when played alongside other tracks. This is done through the use of extreme compression and limiting, and it's a depressing trend that results in much of today's music suffering from a deficit of dynamic range and life.

While there's certainly nothing wrong with running your mix into a compressor on the master output, we'd urge you to exercise some restraint with that level fader and make a point of keeping some dynamic light and shade in your mix.

Above: Your music doesn't have to be super loud to get its point across.

LISTEN IN THE CAR

While it's obviously essential that your mix sounds fantastic through high-quality speakers, it also needs to sound great on lesser systems. One particularly good testing ground for this is a (decent) car stereo. Although it should never be taken as your primary reference, many engineers consider in-car checking an important part of the mixing process.

CAREFUL WITH THAT EQ

We've mentioned it a few times throughout this book, but it bears repeating: don't overdo your EQ, particularly when boosting. If you're in any doubt as to the effect a frequency boost is having, take a break and come back to it later. If you're still in doubt after that, pull it back.

MONITOR WITH HEADPHONES

Most of the time, you should monitor through a high-quality set of studio monitors, but it's worth investing in a good pair of headphones too, and using them periodically to check quieter details that might not be fully apparent through speakers.

Above: Headphones should be secondary to your monitors.

Hot Tip

A strange but tried and tested engineering trick is to listen to the mix from the control room doorway, or just outside it. For some reason, this makes dodgy level variations particularly easy to spot.

DON'T MONITOR TOO LOUD

The vast majority of the time, you should monitor at a moderate volume level, for two reasons. Firstly, your ears won't fatigue as quickly (*see* page 104); second, you won't get the false impression that your mix is perhaps better than it actually is through it simply being louder. Of course, you should crank the volume up now and then, but don't make loud your default.

TURN OFF THE SCREEN

The shapes, colours, playhead and meter movement, and general visuals of your DAW's GUI can have a surprisingly profound effect on your perception of a mix, and even detrimentally influence your engineering decisions on occasion. Listen back to your work-in-progress at regular intervals with the screen turned off — mixing is meant to be about the music, after all!

Above: Watching the mix can skew your perception of it, so turn that screen off!

CHECK THE MIX IN MONO

With more and more people listening to music through their laptop, phone and tablet speakers (the heathens!), and many club systems feeding to one front-of-house channel, your mix needs to sound good in mono. Your DAW is bound to feature a plug-in for real-time conversion of the master out to mono, so don't forget to use it.

VISUAL ANALYSERS

Spectrum analysers, goniometers and other visual analysis tools can prove invaluable when mixing, particularly if your speakers and room aren't able to give the full story with regards to stereo imaging, low-frequency content, phase issues, etc. Your DAW probably has at least a spectrum analyser built in, but check out the likes of iZotope Insight and Blue Cat Audio's various analysis plug-ins if you need something more comprehensive.

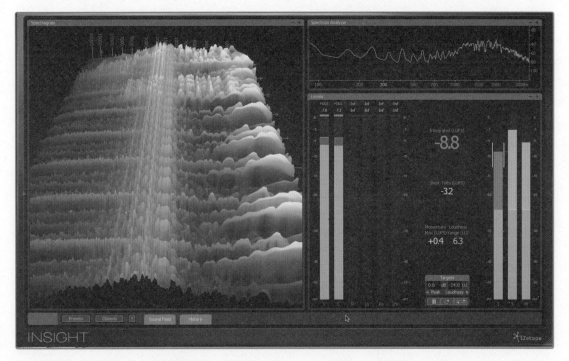

Above: iZotope Insight gives you various flavours of signal analysis.

MASTERING

MASTERING BASICS

Your mix is complete and ready for mastering, but before you fire up that audio editor, there are some things to be considered.

WHAT IS MASTERING?

Mastering is the final stage in preparing a track (or album of tracks) for release. Originally describing the mechanical process of lathing a master disc from a live or tape-recorded signal for duplication, it soon became – and very much still is – a vital part of the creative process. Mastering primarily involves the extremely careful application of EQ, dynamics and stereo image processing, as well as rendering to a final stereo file. It might also entail the use of reverb, noise reduction and even manual correction of audible errors (clicks, pops, etc).

Although there's a strong case for saying that mastering should really be done by a professional mastering engineer (see page 125), there's no reason not to have a go at it yourself, since your DAW or audio editor will include all the tools required.

Left: Mastering was once the purely technical process of pressing tracks to disc.

PREPARING YOUR MIX FOR MASTERING

With your mix finished and ready to master, it needs to be exported from your DAW as a stereo audio file. Whether you're handing it over to a pro engineer or mastering it yourself, there are a few things that need to be kept in mind before you bounce or render it:

1. Leave a few seconds of silent lead-in and lead-out at the start and end, giving the engineer room to manoeuvre in terms of fades in and out.

2. Be absolutely sure that the master output doesn't clip (i.e., exceed 0 dBFS) at any point in the bounce. A peak level of -3 dBFS is a good target to aim for.

3. If you've got any compression, limiting and/or EQ on the master output, it's usually a good idea to turn it off before bouncing/rendering, as the mastering engineer will want to apply their own.

Below: Turn off your master effects before rendering the mix for mastering.

EXPORTING THE MIX

Always export your mix at the exact same sample rate and bit depth as the DAW project itself – ideally, this will be at least 24-bit/48 kHz, and it must never be less than 16-bit/44.1 kHz.

Should you render your stereo WAV or AIF file offline (i.e., as an internal process, much faster than real time) or bounce it in real time? Obviously, if your DAW only offers one or the other, the decision is made for you; and if your project

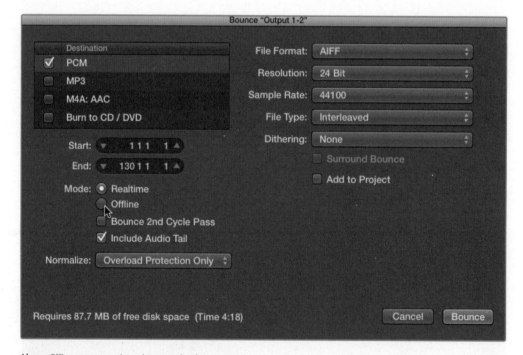

Hot Tip

Whether you real-time bounce or offline export, the end result should be the same. If you're unsure, try both – you won't be able to tell the difference when you listen back to them.

Above: Offline export or real-time bounce – the choice is yours!

includes any external effects processors or MIDI-triggered instruments, real-time bouncing (or manual loopback recording if your DAW doesn't offer it) is your only option.

EASY DOES IT

We can't say this emphatically enough: be cautious and considered with any master processing that you bring to bear on your lovingly crafted mix. By and large, heavy compression, drastic EQ boosts and other profound sonic changes shouldn't be necessary at this stage – unless you're intentionally going for a particular sound that requires them. You should be enhancing an already good mix with your mastering moves, not fixing major issues with a bad one. If you find that you're doing the latter, go back a step and revisit the mix.

Bad mastering can absolutely ruin a good mix, so err on the side of caution at all times, and be sure to keep your un-mastered mix backed up and safe so that you can return to it whenever necessary.

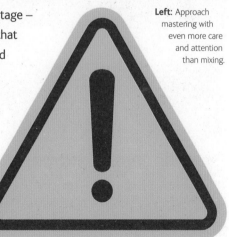

Left: Approach mastering with even more care and attention than mixing.

MASTERING DYNAMICS AND EQUALIZATION

Compression, limiting and EQ are the most important of all mastering tools.

MULTIBAND COMPRESSION AND LIMITING

Take frequency-based control of your dynamics and get your master really pumping.

Multiband Compression

1. The multiband compressor enables you to compress separate frequency ranges by different amounts, giving a very high level of control over the dynamics of the track. With our stereo mix open in an audio editor (Steinberg WaveLab), we load a multiband compressor plug-in.

2. The plug-in splits the input signal into four width-adjustable frequency bands, each processed by its own compressor. By tweaking each band, we can apply heavier compression to the bass frequencies than the vocals, for example, or raise the average level of a kick drum without affecting the snare.

Left: Multiband compression lets you process user-set frequency ranges independently.

Limiting

Limiting is used at the mastering stage to increase the perceived loudness of the track by reducing its dynamic range. We discussed limiting in depth on page 65, so we won't get into the details again here, but we will repeat our call to exercise restraint

Above: If the meters on your master limiter look like this, you might be overdoing it.

with it. Dynamics are vitally important in most forms of music, so while driving your mix hard into a brick-wall limiter might make it commercially competitive, it will also invariably compromise the quality and sensitivity of the track. Ask yourself if that's really an acceptable trade-off.

MASTERING EQ

The careful use of equalization can add air and space to your master.

> ## Hot Tip
>
> **Audio editors like Steinberg WaveLab feature pen tools that let you draw pops and glitches out of the waveform. If you can re-render the mix without the offending error though, that's always the preferred solution.**

Applying Mastering EQ

1. Like compression, EQ at the mastering stage can do more harm than good if not handled delicately. With our mix in WaveLab once again, we load FabFilter Pro-Q 2.

2. Switching Pro-Q 2 to Linear Phase mode (and Max quality) ensures minimal phase distortion, with an increase in latency that doesn't matter, since we're not recording anything. (*See* page 118 for more on this.)

3. With our track having been mixed correctly to achieve good tonal balance, our mastering EQ adjustments are aimed at sweetening the mix rather than significantly changing it. A lot of A/B bypassing is done, and we give ourselves a few hours' break from the track before listening to it with fresh ears and committing to our tweaks.

LINEAR PHASE EQ

As well as adjusting the volume levels of specific frequencies in a signal, conventional minimum phase EQ plug-ins also change the phase of those frequencies. This means that some frequencies end up appearing at the output later than others.

With individual sounds, these imperceptible delays don't matter. In the context of mastering though, where audio fidelity is paramount and any processing imperfections can't be buried in the mix, they can be troublesome.

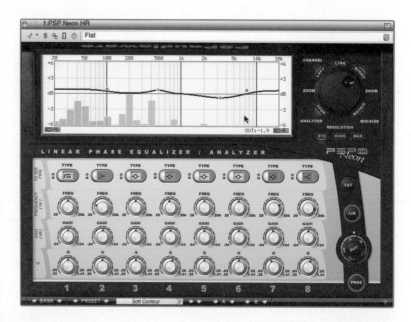

Linear phase EQ (examples include PSP Audioware Neon HR, FabFilter Pro-Q 2 and Blue Cat Audio Liny EQ) exhibit a linear phase response, with all frequencies arriving at the same time, albeit at the cost of latency, higher CPU usage and so-called pre-ringing artefacts.

Left: PSP's Neon HR is a linear phase EQ perfectly suited to mastering.

OTHER MASTERING PROCESSES

Dynamics and EQ form the core of your mastering effects set-up, but there are a few other things you can add to it too.

MASTERING REVERB

Very subtle reverb can be used to boost the ambience and air in spacious acoustic tracks, or bring a positive depth-enhancing, gluing effect to denser mixes. Use the highest-quality plug-in you have (start with a convolution model), keep the wet/dry mix below 20 per cent wet, and use a low-pass filter to cut everything below 150 Hz or so out of the reverb. If you're using it to apply depth and glue, ditch everything above 3 kHz, too. Mastering reverb isn't meant to be obviously audible – your actual reverb should be applied as part of the mixing process.

Below: If you're going to apply mastering reverb, make sure you use a top-notch plug-in, such as Audio Ease Altiverb.

STEREO IMAGING

Although achieving a wide but controlled stereo panorama is
something that should be happening during mixdown, further spatial
adjustment is often carried out by the mastering engineer.

Mid/side processing (see page 46) is a powerful ally, here, enabling
the centre of the image to be tightened and the edges to be pulled
inwards or pushed outwards. Use a dedicated mid/side processor for
this, or a compressor, EQ, etc., with a mid/side mode.

There are also plenty of plug-ins dedicated to stereo imaging, many
of them aimed specifically at mastering.

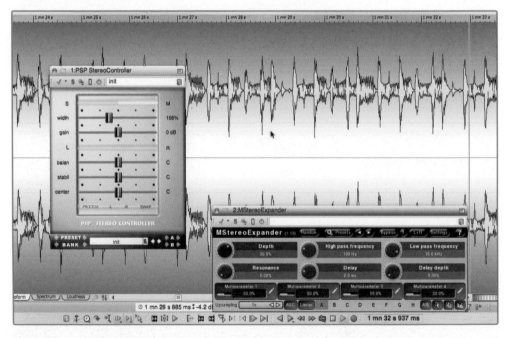

Above: Stereo imaging plug-ins might not be exciting, but they certainly come in handy for mastering.

EXCITERS

If your mix is lacking in top-end sparkle and shimmer, the application of an exciter plug-in at the mastering stage can make for an effective cure when additive EQ just isn't getting the job done.

Excitement differs from EQ in that the latter boosts the level of existing frequencies – thus potentially raising background noise or the edges of immediately adjacent frequencies – while the former uses a combination of distortion, dynamic EQ and other processes to actually add harmonics based on the material already present.

With the ear being so sensitive to high-frequency sounds, over-exuberant use of excitement can result in a master that's harsh, unbalanced and tiring to listen to – so don't overdo it, if you use it at all.

MASTERING SUITES

If you're really serious about getting into mastering, there are some deeply impressive software packages available that put all of the processors discussed in this chapter (and more) under one virtual roof.

The most famous and probably most powerful mastering suite of all is iZotope Ozone, currently at version 6. The Advanced edition makes its comprehensive line-up of modules

Above: T-RackS has always been a solid choice for mastering.

accessible together in a standalone application, or individually as plug-ins. Other great options include IK Multimedia T-RackS CS (which started life many years ago as a dedicated mastering system and still does a sterling job in that role, despite its recently broadened remit), and bundles by the likes of Waves, Sonnox and FabFilter.

THE FINAL MASTER

With your final processing applied and lead-in/out times set, your master is ready for the world to hear.

EXPORTING THE MASTER

There are a few things to consider before you hit that Render button.

Sample Rate, Bit Depth and Dither

Although CD is no longer the essential target medium it once was, CD-quality remains the universal format of choice for mastering. So, that's 16-bit/44.1 kHz, which strikes a good balance between file size and audio fidelity.

If your exported master is at a lower bit depth than the original mix (dropping from 24-bit to 16-bit), you may want to apply dither. Dither is very quiet noise added to the signal to conceal the low-level distortion that comes when reducing bit depth. Your DAW or audio editor may offer a range of dither types (triangular, square, etc.), so spend some time researching and trying them to gain an understanding of the differences.

File Compression

As well as 16-bit WAV or AIF, you'll probably need to export your master in one or more compressed formats, depending on what distribution services and systems you have in mind for it.

Export to MP3, AAC, OGG, etc. should be done in parallel with your main render, rather than from it. You should compress your original 24-bit mix (with the exact same master processing in place as the main WAV/AIF master) rather than your processed, dithered 16-bit master. This ensures optimum audio quality by minimizing the number of file conversion stages.

Hot Tip

Some DAWs and audio editors let you render multiple formats (WAV and MP3, for example) at once, which can simplify and speed up the export process.

Below: Export MP3 directly from the processed source mix, rather than the rendered master.

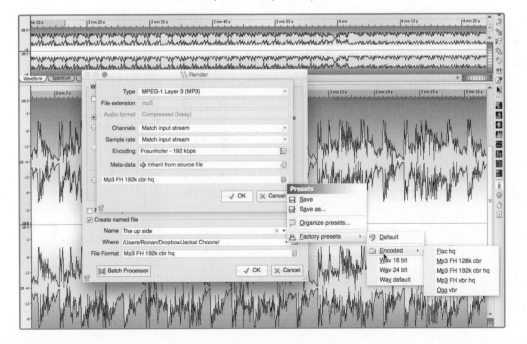

A/B REFERENCING

Just like when mixing, A/B comparison of your track with a commercial release (that you admire the sound of) throughout the mastering session is a must – even the most seasoned pros do it. The goal isn't necessarily to precisely copy the sound of the reference, but rather to generally match it in terms of frequency distribution, punch, imaging and feel.

There's even a plug-in available to streamline the A/B workflow. Sample Magic's Magic AB lets you instantly compare your master (or mix – it's equally useful at that stage too) with up to six reference tracks at the click of a mouse, saving you from having to flip between your audio editor or DAW and your media player.

Below: Sample Magic's Magic AB is a unique and uniquely useful plug-in.

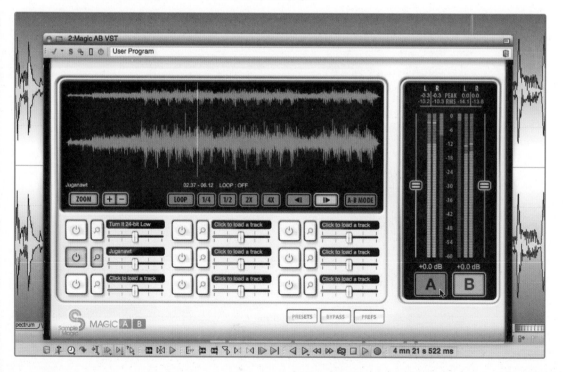

Above: If you really want your track to sound its best, get it professionally mastered.

WHY PROFESSIONAL MASTERING IS WORTH PAYING FOR

Having taken you through the fundamentals of mastering, we'd be remiss if we didn't conclude by saying that it really is a job best left to the professionals.

It takes years of experience, a highly trained ear, a beautifully treated room full of ridiculously expensive gear, and a lot of deep technical know-how to get to grips with mastering. It really isn't something you can just throw yourself into without knowing what you're doing in the hope that you'll get lucky.

So, until you develop your ears and skills through practice, we have to recommend that you get your mixes finalized by a professional mastering engineer, of which there are an increasing number offering their services online at very reasonable rates. Your tracks will sound better for it, and you'll learn a lot by hearing your own music mastered properly.

USEFUL WEBSITES AND FURTHER READING

WEBSITES

www.dogsonacid.com
Forum for sharing material and discussing topics related to electronic music and Drum & Bass.

www.em411.com
Collection of blogs where users can publish and discuss their own and others' work, including audio tracks, equipment reviews and guidance on techniques.

www.futureproducers.com/forums/
Large online community providing insight into the best technologies and techniques within the world of music production.

www.gearslutz.com
Forum for sharing information about audio recording and production techniques.

www.harmonycentral.com
Handy resource for musicians, featuring news, product reviews and a forum space.

www.kvraudio.com
Community and news site for audio plug-in and mobile app users.

wwww.musicradar.com
News site for the music industry, where experts review the latest music equipment and provide tips, projects and video tutorials.

www.musictech.net
Website dedicated to the latest trends, techniques, gear and software in the industry, featuring tutorials, reviews and news updates.

www.sonicstate.com
A hub for electronic musicians that includes digital music equipment resources, reviews and ratings, a database of synthesizers and an online community space.

www.soundonsound.com
Online articles from the music recording technology magazine, with additional product demonstrations, tutorials and interviews from experts in the field.

FURTHER READING

Cutchin, Rusty *Apple Logic Pro Basics*, Flame Tree Publishing Ltd, 2015

Clewes, Dave, *Avid Pro Tools Basics*, Flame Tree Publishing Ltd, 2015

Cutchin, Rusty, *Music Theory for Computer Musicians*, Flame Tree Publishing Ltd, 2015

Gilreath, Paul, *The Guide to MIDI Orchestration: 4th Edition*, Focal Press, 2010

Hewitt, Michael, *Harmony for Computer Musicians*, Alfred Publishing, 2010

Pohlmann, Ken C., *Principles of Digital Audio*, Sixth Edition, Tab Electronics, 2010

Reiss, Joshua D. and McPherson, Andrew, *Audio Effects: Theory, Implementation and Application*, CRC Press, 2014

Senior, Mike, *Mixing Secrets for the Small Studio*, Focal Press, 2011

INDEX